PIANO · VOCAL · GUITAR

MICHAEL

T0059225

Produced by
Alfred Music Publishing Co., Inc.
P.O. Box 10003
Van Nuys, CA 91410-0003
alfred.com

Printed in USA.

ISBN-10: 0-7390-7889-5
ISBN-13: 978-0-7390-7889-1

© 2010 MJJ Productions Inc. / ℗ 2010 MJJ Productions.

CONTENTS

HOLLYWOOD TONIGHT

Written and Composed by
MICHAEL JACKSON and BRADLEY BUXER

Moderately ♩ = 112

1.3. Lip - stick in hand, Ta - hi - tian tanned,   in her paint-ed on____
2. West - bound Grey - hound to Tin-sel-town to pur-sue her mov-ie - star____

____ jeans.____
____ dreams.____   She's giv - ing

Nothing more she could want, she was determined to follow her plan.

She wanted Hollywood. She wanted it bad.

Now that she caught her dream, she became a star.

And it all looked so good, but only good from afar.

Imprisoned in every paparazzi's camera. Every guy wished they could.

HOLD MY HAND

Words and Music by
CLAUDE KELLY, AKON and GIORGIO TUINFORT

*Recorded in D♭ major.

Hold My Hand - 12 - 1

so tell me what we're wait - ing for?

Hold my hand.

We're bet-ter off be - ing to - geth - er

Hold my hand.

than be-ing mis - 'ra - ble a - lone. 'Cause

Hold my hand.

12

I've been there be-fore and you've been there be-fore, but to-geth-er, we can be al - right. 'Cause

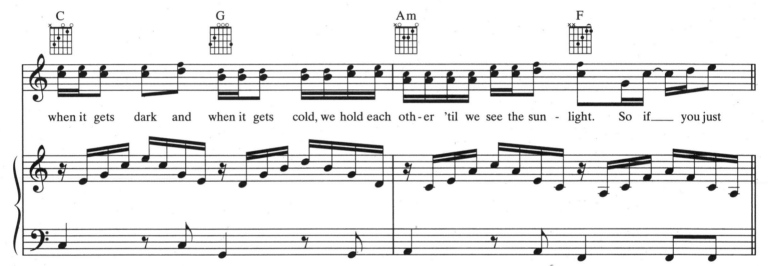

when it gets dark and when it gets cold, we hold each oth-er 'til we see the sun - light. So if___ you just

Chorus:

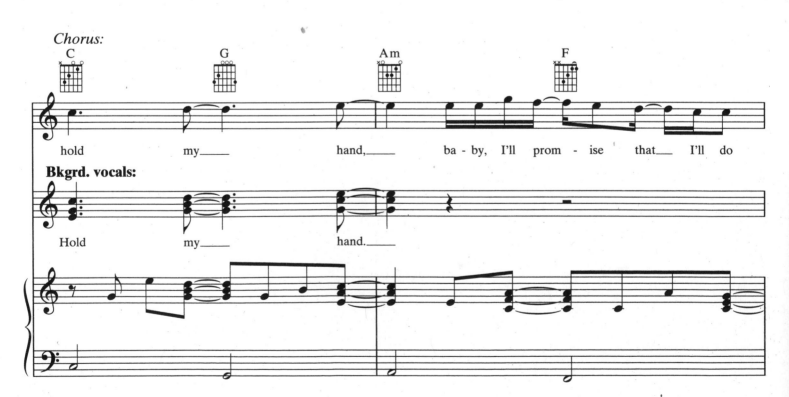

hold my___ hand,___ ba - by, I'll prom - ise that___ I'll do

Bkgrd. vocals:

Hold my___ hand.___

all   I   can,_____   things will go bet - ter if____ you just

All   I_____   can.

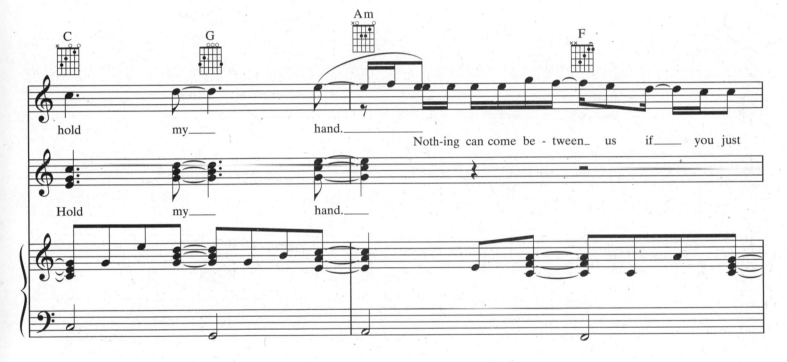

hold   my___   hand._____   Noth-ing can come be - tween_ us if____ you just

Hold   my___   hand._____

hold my,   hold my,   hold_ my hand.   Hold_ my hand._

Hold my,   hold my,   hold_ my hand.

Verse 2:

16 *Chorus:*

hold my_____ hand,_____ ba - by, I'll prom - ise that___ I'll do

Hold my_____ hand.____

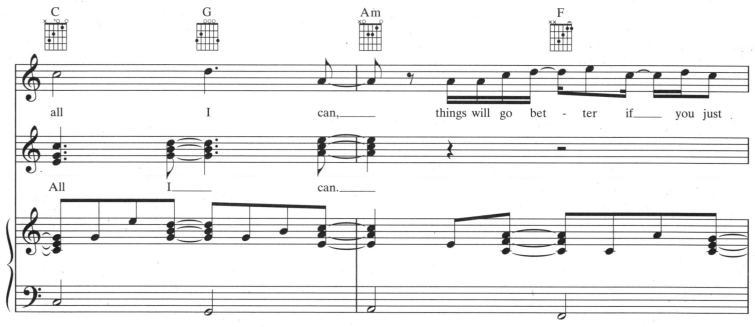

all I can,_____ things will go bet - ter if____ you just

All I____ can.____

hold my_____ hand.____ Noth-ing can come be - tween_ us if____ you just

Hold my_____ hand.____

Verse 3:

19

20

Whoo!   Whoo!   Whoo!   Whoo! Hold__ my

Hold my,   hold my,   hold__ my hand.

hand._____   Mm._____

_____   *(Whispered:) Hold my hand.*

rall.

KEEP YOUR HEAD UP

Written and Composed by
MICHAEL JACKSON, EDDIE CASCIO
and JAMES PORTE

Verse 1 (sing 1st time only):

1. She's look-ing for a job and to find a place_ to stay.___ She's

Verse 2 (sing 2nd time only):

kill-ing up the life in the birds and___ the trees.___ And we're

Keep Your Head Up - 9 - 1

(I LIKE) THE WAY YOU LOVE ME

Written and Composed by
MICHAEL JACKSON

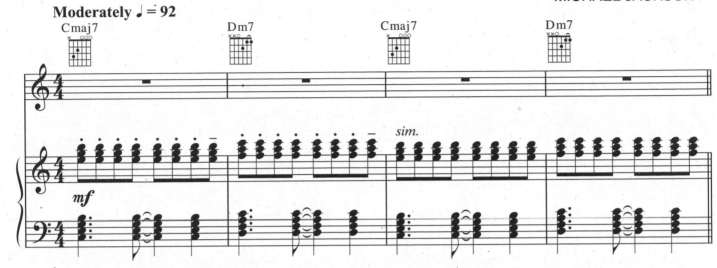

Verse 1:

1. I was a-lone in the dark when I met ya, woo.

You took my hand and you told me you loved me, woo.

38

Amaj7

I like the way how you hold-

Chorus:

Amaj7

Bm7

in' me.
It does-n't mat-ter how you are hold-ing me.

I like the way how you lov-

Amaj7

Bm7

in' me.
It does-n't mat-ter how you are lov-ing me.

I like the way how you touch-

Amaj7

Bm7

in' me.
It does-n't mat-ter how you are touch-ing me.

I like the way how you kiss-

(I Like) the Way You Love Me - 9 - 9

MONSTER

Written and Composed by
MICHAEL JACKSON, EDDIE CASCIO,
JAMES PORTE and CURTIS JACKSON

Moderately, with a strong beat ♩ = 96

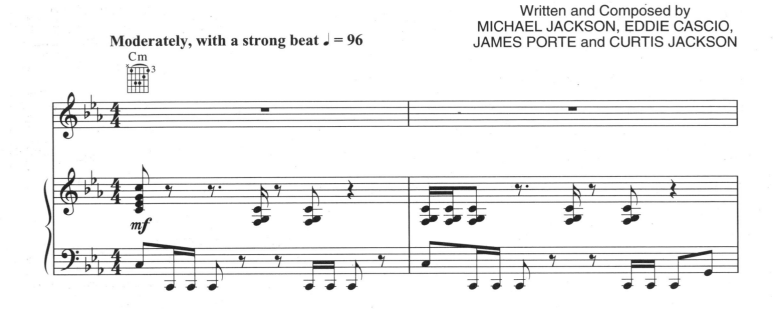

Monster - 8 - 1

Verses 1 & 2:

1. You can look at them com-in' out the walls. You can look at them climb-in' out the bush-es.
(2.) com-in' at ya, com-in' at ya rath-er too fast. Ma-ma say you ma-ma got you in a zig zag.

You can find them when the let-ter's 'bout to fall. He be wait-in' with his cam-'ra right on fo-cus.
And you're run-nin' and you're run-nin' just to 'scape it. But they're gun-nin' for the mon-ey, so they fake it.

Ev-'ry-where you seem to turn, there's a mon-ster. When you look up in the air, there's a mon-ster.
Ev-'ry-where you seem to turn, there's a mon-ster. When you look up in the air, there's a mon-ster.

N.C.

Pa-pa-raz-zi got you scared like a mon-ster, mon-ster, mon-ster. } Too bad,
When you see them in the street, that's a mon-ster, mon-ster, mon-ster. }

Chorus:

Mon - ster, he's a mon - ster, he's an an - i - mal.__

Mon - ster, he's a

To Coda ⊕

mon - ster, he's an an - i - mal,_____

|1.

ho._____

|2.

2. He's oo._____

Bridge:

Why are they__ nev - er sat - is - fied__ with and

all you give?__ Ha, you give them your all,___

__ they're watch - ing you fall,_____ and they

eat your soul_____ like a veg - 'ta - ble.
(Spoken:) Yeah, yeah, yeah.

Verses 3 & 4:

3. *Catch me in a bad mood, flippin'; you'll take a whippin'.*   *Animal, Hannibal, cannibal addition.*
4. *All hell, run tell, the King has risen.*   *2010 Thriller, there's nothing iller, it's killer.*

Tears appear, yeah, blurring your vision.   *Fear in the air, screaming, your blood drippin'.*
Their vision, the missin' one, the pack, this is that.   *It's the bomb, ring the alarm. MJ Number One.*

1.

Shiver a second, now, now, now, now, what is it?   *Funerals, cemeteries; don't worry, it's time to visit.*

Broke bones, tombstones, who do you think I'm kiddin'?   *It's home, sweet home, the land of the forbidden.*

mon - ster,   he's an   an - i - mal.   He's

drag - gin' you   down like a mon - ster.   He's drag - gin' you   down like a mon - ster.

1.

2.

BEST OF JOY

Written and Composed by
MICHAEL JACKSON

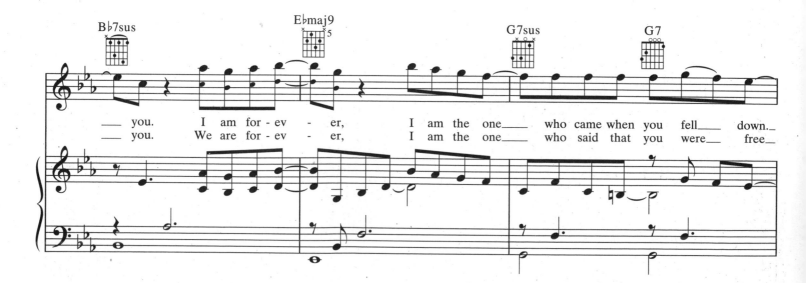

Lyrics line 1: 1. I am your joy,____ your best of joy.____ I am the moon-

Lyrics line 2: through thick and thin,____ we need each oth-

light, you are the spring, our love's a sa-cred thing. You know I al-ways will love_

er, we'll nev-er part. Our love is from the heart. We nev-er say I don't need_

____ you. I am for-ev—er, I am the one____ who came when you fell____ down.__

____ you. We are for-ev—er, I am the one____ who said that you were____ free__

Best of Joy - 4 - 1

BREAKING NEWS

Written and Composed by
MICHAEL JACKSON, EDDIE CASCIO
and JAMES PORTE

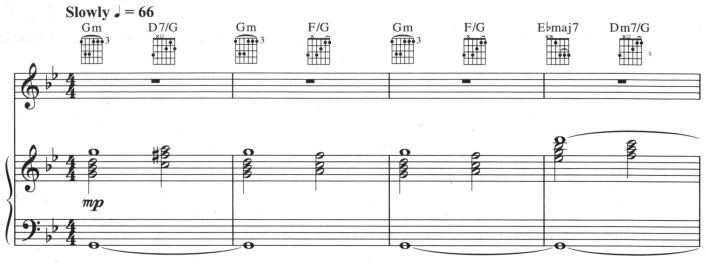

Breaking news.

Breaking News - 6 - 1

Verse:
Gm

1. Ev - 'ry - bod - y want-ing a piece___ of Mi-chael Jack - son.___ Re - port - ers stalk -ing the moves_
2. Ev - 'ry - bod - y watch-ing the news___ on Mi-chael Jack - son.___ They wan - na see that I fall,_

___ of Mi-chael Jack - son.___ Just when you thought he was done,___ he comes to give it a - gain._
___ 'cause I'm Mi-chael Jack - son.___ You write the words to de - stroy,___ like it's a wea-pon.

___ They can put it a-round the world_ to - day. He wan-na write my o - bit - u - ar - y.___
You turned your back on the love____ and you can't get it a - gain._

54

No mat - ter what, you just wan - na read it a - gain.___ No mat - ter what,

Chorus:

you just wan - na feed it a - gain.___ Why is it strange that I would fall in love?___

Who is that boog - ey - man you're think - ing of?___ Or am I cra - zy 'cause I

1.

just in - dulge?___ This is break - ing news.___ This is break -
(They keep break-ing the news.

56

D.S. ℅ al Coda

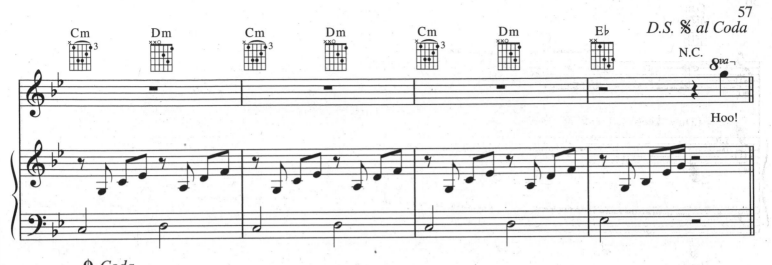

Hoo!

Coda

(They keep break-ing the news.)
ing news.___

Hee hee hee.

Hee hee hee hee.   You're break-ing   the news.

(I CAN'T MAKE IT) ANOTHER DAY

Words and Music by
LENNY KRAVITZ

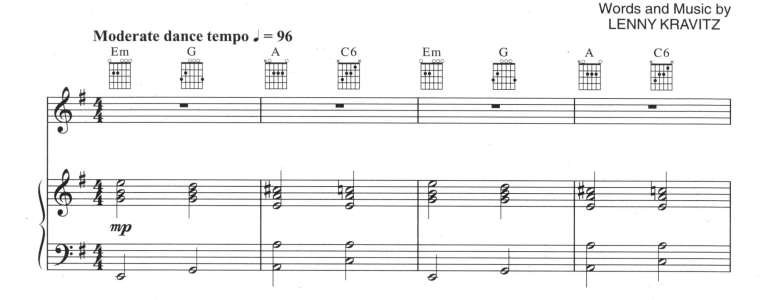

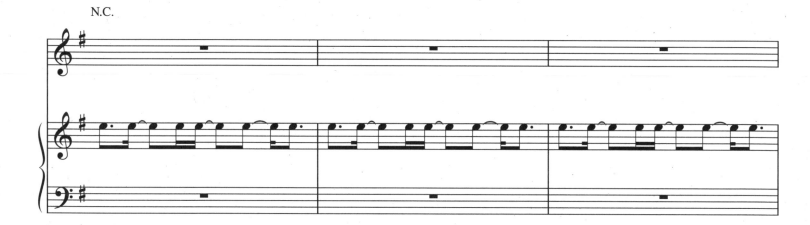

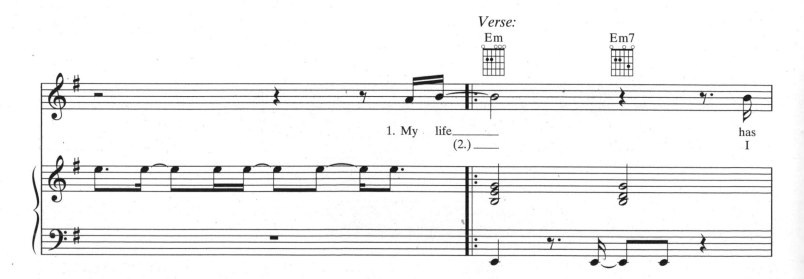

1. My life_____ has I
(2.) _____

(I Can't Make It) Another Day - 7 - 2

60

live an - oth - er day___ with - out___ your love.___

(I Can't Make It) Another Day - 7 - 6

63

64

BEHIND THE MASK

Written and Composed by
MICHAEL JACKSON, CHRIS MOSDELL
and RYUICHI SAKAMOTO

Moderately ♩ = 108

(Sax. solo...

...end solo)

N.C.

a tempo

mf

Verse 1:

1. All a-long, I had___ to talk a-bout it.

Behind the Mask - 7 - 1

66

MUCH TOO SOON

Written and Composed by
MICHAEL JACKSON

74

Much Too Soon - 5 - 3